PENGUIN BOOKS

Matt Roper is a feature writer for British tabloid the *Daily Mirror*. He lived in Brazil for six years, where he managed to survive tarantula attacks, falling coconuts and swimming in piranha-infested waters in the Amazon jungle. He also infiltrated a Bolivian drug gang to investigate child prostitution rings, and dodged bullets to report on death squads in Rio de Janeiro. He returned to the UK after setting up a project for street girls in one of Brazil's biggest cities. He now lives in London with his wife Daniela. He has written two other books, *Street Girls* and *Remember Me, Rescue Me*.

101 CRAZY WAYS TO DIE

MATT ROPER

PENGUIN BOOKS

INTRODUCTION

Do you know what the chances are of you reaching the end of this page alive?

Well, pretty good, all things considered. Unless, that is, you're standing outside a Baghdad police station, on the deck of an arctic fishing trawler or laid flat in a hospital bed surrounded by sobbing relatives . . . in which case, put the book down!

Even the odds of you surviving until the end of this book are reasonably high (assuming you're not a terribly slow reader).

Then again, if you're reading this while soaking up the sun on some tropical beach, there's always that outside chance you could get knocked off by a falling coconut, washed to a watery grave by a freak wave or stung to death by a swarm of killer bees.

Even if you're minding your own business on a park bench somewhere, you might suddenly be crushed by a falling aeroplane engine, smashed to smithereens by a meteorite or vapourised in a nuclear explosion.

There are a million-and-one ways to die, from the mundane to the plain insane, from the seriously sad to the downright hilarious (but don't laugh too much – people have died from that too). But of course most of us don't go around worrying about whether we're about to get killed by a stray golf ball, or impaled by a falling icicle, because what are the chances of that?

So why the rush of paralysing fear every time the plane hurtles down the runway, the panic-stricken palpitations as the rollercoaster climbs skywards, or the jelly legs as you cross that 300-metre-high (900-foot-high) bridge that's been there for years?

You probably refuse to go swimming in the ocean for fear of what might be lurking beneath, but I bet you have no problems lazing on a sun-soaked beach, relaxing in a soothing bath or sleeping in your bed – where statistically you're more likely to come a cropper.

In fact, you're much more likely to get killed by the work photocopier than the neighbourhood nuclear reactor, or waiting for the bus than blown up by a suicide bomber . . . so why do we worry ourselves to death about things that will probably never happen?

Well, you can finally put your irrational fears to bed. We've tracked down the odds of you succumbing to everything from a sneezing fit to a spider bite, and everything in between. You'll soon realise that the causes of death you've been most afraid of are actually very unlikely to occur.

For instance, did you know that you're more likely to meet your maker sitting on the loo than on the loop-the-loop? Or that there's more chance you'll be washed out to sea while standing on dry land than go down with a sinking cruise liner? Or that more people are killed each year by cow dung than ripped apart by man-eating sharks?

And, finally, if you bought a lottery ticket today, remember that your chances of becoming a millionaire are about the same as getting frazzled by a bolt of lightning, trampled by a charging elephant or dying before you reach the end of this page.

Well done, you've made it!

LEFT-HANDED PERSON USING A RIGHT-HANDED PRODUCT

4.4 million to one

More than 3000 left-handed people are killed every year by equipment meant for right-handed people, with the right-handed power saw being the most deadly item.

Research also shows that left-handed people are poorer judges of distance, making them more vulnerable to car crashes and other serious accidents. It may explain why right-handed people live, on average, nine years longer than lefties.

LAWNMOWER

10 million to one

Around 180 000 people are injured in lawnmower accidents every year. In May 2005, a 59-year-old woman died while cutting the grass at her property in Wang, Austria, when she fell on a slope and her electric lawnmower rolled back on top of her.

A year earlier, another Austrian died when he mowed over a discarded shotgun cartridge which detonated, causing the petrol tank to explode, sending the 40-year-old man flying backwards and landing on his head.

DISHWASHER

280 million to one

It is supposed to take away one of life's dullest chores – but dishwashers aren't always good news, especially if they're packed with kitchen knives.

In May 2003, a 31-year-old woman from Lanarkshire, Scotland, died after she slipped in her kitchen and landed on a knife sitting upright in the dishwasher which pierced through her heart. It is a tragedy which has been repeated a disturbing number of times in recent years, with safety groups even issuing warnings about always putting knives face down in dishwashers.

FALLING THROUGH A FROZEN LAKE

6.6 million to one

Every year hundreds of people die after falling through frozen lakes and rivers.

In Britain, at least five people drown every year under ice-covered lakes – most while trying to rescue their dogs. In 1996, a husband and wife from Upminster, Essex, died trying to save their black Labrador, Tara, from an Essex lake. Tara later swam out unharmed.

SLEEPWALKING

42 million to one

In 2005, a 15-year-old girl from London was rescued after sleepwalking to the top of a 40-metre (80 foot) crane near her home. However, dozens of others who walk off hotel balconies or across busy motorways while fast asleep aren't so lucky.

In Sydney, Australia, one hotel has banned sleepwalkers' conventions because of the number of conventioneers hurting themselves – and damaging property – during the early hours.

And in 1997, a 14-year-old boy got out of bed and sleepwalked, like he often did, to the kitchen. He sleepwalked out the kitchen door – of the family's RV, which was barrelling down a San Diego highway at the time.

TRIPPING OVER

150 000 to one

More than 2000 people die from tripping or slipping over every year in the United States alone.

In August 2001, a 28-year-old New Zealander died in a freak accident when he slipped on ice while feeding his cat, was knocked unconscious and drowned in the cat's water bowl.

FACT

In November 2005, 16-year-old Li Xiao Meng, a budding guitarist from China, got so carried away while bouncing on his bed mimicking a rock star that he flew out his window and fell three floors to his death.

FACT

Twenty-three-year-old Scott Kell, a karate brown belt and Thai boxing enthusiast, lost his balance doing high kicks and plunged to his death through an open window on the 10th floor of a tower block in Salford, England, in 1994.

10

FALLING OUT OF BED

3 million to one

In Britain, around 20 people die after falling out of bed every year, and another 20 die after falling over while getting out of bed. In the United States, bed falls account for 1.8 million emergency room visits and 400 000 hospital admissions a year.

In August 2005, two English sisters in their sixties were sound asleep in a bed in the Spanish resort of Benidorm, when the pull-down bed frame fell on top of them. Police said they had made desperate attempts to free themselves before being suffocated.

MURDER WHILE SLEEPING

45 million to one

There have been at least 68 cases worldwide of murder while sleeping. In 1982, a man stabbed his wife 25 times with a kitchen knife – but was cleared by an American judge because he was sleepwalking when he did it.

And in 1999, a man in British Columbia, Canada, claimed he was sleepwalking when he stabbed his wife 47 times, hid the body, grabbed some money and a change of clothes then flew to Mexico where, he claimed, he woke up. For some reason the jury didn't believe him.

VIAGRA

8 million to one

Since it was launched in 1998, over 5600 men have died after taking the anti-impotence pill Viagra.

In 1998, Nigerian dictator Sani Abacha ended up stiff – but not in the way he'd intended – after a heart attack, rumoured to have been caused by taking large quantities of the drug before taking part in an orgy.

FACT

Forty-five-year-old Dr Oscar Dominguez, a psychiatrist in Sao Paulo, Brazil, admitted he'd shot and killed his patient while she told him about her sex life. He told the court, 'I couldn't take those nut cases anymore'.

HAVING AN AFFAIR
850 000 to one (if you're the one who's cheating)

Men face twice the normal risk of having a heart attack after making love, but this increases further for men who are cheating on their wives. Men who are having an affair with a younger woman are most at risk.

ENERGY DRINKS
118 million to one

Some energy drinks contain as much as 200 mg (.007 oz) of caffeine, which is enough to trigger a heart attack in people with pre-existing heart conditions. Even in the young and healthy, the drinks, which are banned in France and Belgium, can cause palpitations and send blood pressure soaring.

In 2003, a healthy, 18-year-old basketball player from Limerick, Ireland, collapsed on the court and died after drinking four cans before a basketball game.

And in 2006, a man was charged and jailed for four months for dangerous driving after drinking around 20 cans of an energy drink. His car was seen 'swerving from side to side' along a major road in Norfolk, England.

KINKY SEX
1.2 million to one

In 1994, British Conservative MP Stephen Milligan died as a result of autoerotic asphyxiation – the practice of cutting off oxygen to the brain during sex, to experience a heightened state of pleasure. It is a fate shared by some 5000 people around the world each year.

FACT

Shy couple Sachi and Tomio Hidaka of Chiba, Japan, waited 14 years before making love for the first time in 1992. It proved too much and both died of heart attacks, although neither had a history of heart trouble.

CHAMPAGNE CORK

83 million to one

More people are killed each year by flying champagne corks than bites from poisonous spiders. Of the nearly two dozen champagne-accident fatalities a year, over a third occur at weddings – a surefire way of turning a toast into a tragedy.

WALKING INTO A LAMPPOST

360 million to one

Women are mostly to blame for the 18 000 lamppost-related injuries every year, of which three-quarters of casualties are men. An average of four a year don't survive the collision.

BUMPING INTO SOMEONE

100 million to one

Head-on collisions between pedestrians claim hundreds of lives every year. In the Ukraine, 10 per cent of all accidental deaths are from one person bumping into another in congested areas like market-places or shopping centres.

FALLING OFF A LADDER

2.3 million to one

At least 300 people die from falling off ladders every year, while over half a million suffer serious injuries.

Of course, the person holding the ladder is also at risk. In August 2004, a woman from London died instantly when her husband lost his balance and fell on top of her while using an electric chainsaw.

FALLING AIRCRAFT PART

700 million to one

You're nearly as likely to be hit by aircraft debris as attacked by a shark. A recent study of civil aviation accidents found that, between 1964 and 1999, falling aircraft parts killed an average of eight people per year.

In 1989, a soviet MiG-23 fighter jet, which had escaped on autopilot from Poland after the crew ejected, crashed on top of an oblivious Belgian teenager.

PLANE CRASH

10 million to one

Plane crashes claim 1300 lives every year. Young men are most likely to emerge from the wreckage alive – and 12 per cent of passengers who survive the impact will later die from shock.

SINKING CRUISE LINER

13.5 million to one

Every week, at least one ship sinks to the bottom of the ocean, often without a Mayday call or any explanation as to what happened.

In May 1999, the *Sun Vista* cruise ship containing 472 passengers – mostly Britons and Australians – caught fire and sank in darkness off the coast of Malaysia. Passengers sang the theme song from the film *Titanic*, 'My Heart Will Go On', to keep up their spirits as the evacuation took place.

FACT

A Brazilian pilot was showing off to his girlfriend by performing loop-the-loops over her house in his Cessna aircraft. At the bottom of one loop, he flew low over the house and shouted 'I love you' to her as he passed – however the wing of his plane clipped the chimney and sent the plane crashing to the ground, killing him instantly.

VENDING MACHINE

380 million to one

At least 40 people in North America have been crushed by toppling vending machines, which can weigh over 408 kg (900 lb) when fully stocked.

In 1998, a Canadian student was trapped underneath a 419 kg (924 lb) Coke machine at his residence hall at Bishop's University, Ontario. It fell on top of him after he rocked it back and forth to get a free can. His body was found by fellow students the next morning.

CAR PARK BARRIER

60 million to one

In 2002, a man from Wales became one of the six unlucky people a year to be killed by car park security barriers. He was killed instantly when a metal supermarket barrier crashed through his windscreen and hit him in the head on a trip to buy a garden shed.

REVOLVING DOOR

512 million to one

They say death is a revolving door – but for some people that's more than just a metaphor. In March 2004, revolving doors killed two children: a six-year-old boy was killed as he and his mother entered an office building in central Tokyo, and an 18-month-old boy was crushed by an automatic revolving door at Cologne airport in Germany.

COMPUTER GAMES

5 million to one

Every year, an increasing number of people die from exhaustion after playing on-line computer games for hours at a stretch.

In October 2002, a Taiwanese man was found bleeding from the nose and foaming at the mouth, after playing computer games non-stop for 32 hours in an Internet cafe. He died before reaching hospital.

Just days earlier, a 24-year-old man died after playing the game *Starcraft* non-stop for 86 hours at an Internet café in South Korea. Interestingly, in South Korea 15 million people are registered for on-line gaming.

TRAPPED IN FREEZER

360 million to one

Some people go to fetch a bag of frozen peas or tub of ice cream from the freezer and never come back.

In 2006, the 19-year-old assistant manager of a Haagen-Dazs ice cream parlour died after becoming trapped in the freezer in Stratford-upon-Avon, England.

MOBILE PHONE

720 million to one

You hardly expect to get your head blown off when you answer your mobile phone. According to the United States Safety Commission, 83 mobile phones have exploded without warning in the past few years.

In January 2006, a 59-year-old Californian's mobile exploded in his pocket and started a fire which severely burned half his body and gutted his hotel room.

FACT

In March 1992, Russian chess Grand Master Gudkov outwitted and checkmated a computer three times in a row at a public tournament in Moscow. The next time he touched the machine, however, it electrocuted him and, despite being rushed to hospital, he died.

FACT

In July 1981, Japanese factory worker Kenji Urada became the first known fatality caused by a robot. While repairing a faulty robot at a Kawasaki plant, the 37-year-old maintenance engineer failed to turn it off completely, resulting in the robot pushing him into a grinding machine with its hydraulic arm.

SPACE JUNK

1.3 billion to one

In September 1962, a metal object about 15 cm (6 in) in diameter and weighing 10 kg (22 lb) crashed into a street intersection in Manitowoc, Wisconsin. It burrowed several centimetres into the ground. The object was later identified as part of Sputnik IV, which had been launched by the USSR on 15 May 1960. Since 1959, more than 6000 parts of spacecraft have fallen out of orbit. Many of them have reached the surface of Earth.

In March 2007, a Lan Chile Airlines Airbus flying from Santiago, Chile, to New Zealand had a narrow miss with space junk from what was believed to be a Russian satellite. The concerned pilot saw debris hurtling through the sky only 5 km (3 mi) away from his plane. Flying at 880 km (547 mi) an hour the plane was only 40 seconds away from a potential disaster.

METEORITE

7.5 billion to one

Around 500 space rocks hit the earth every year, but amazingly the only reported fatality is an Egyptian dog that was killed in 1911.

The only known human to be hit by a meteorite was Ann Hodges in Sylacauga, Alabama. In 1954, she was bruised when a 4 kg (9 lb) stone crashed through her living room roof and bounced off her radio.

STRUCK BY LIGHTNING

10 million to one

A lightning bolt has an electrical charge of roughly 100 million volts and is five times hotter than the surface of the sun. It kills around 1000 people a year – men are four times more likely to be struck than women.

In October 1998, all 11 members of a visiting football team were killed by a bolt of lightning during a match in the Congo. Amazingly, every member of the home team escaped unhurt.

FACT

Star Trek creator Gene Roddenberry became the first person to have his ashes blasted into space. In October 1992, astronaut Jim Weatherbee took the ashes with him onboard the space shuttle Columbia and carried out Roddenberry's dying wish. The stainless steel cylinder is still out there somewhere.

EXPLODING TOILET
340 million to one

In 1988, an Israeli housewife found a cockroach in her living room, threw it in the toilet and, when it refused to die, sprayed a full can of insecticide on it. Later, her husband came home from work, sat on the toilet smoking a cigarette, then threw the butt into the bowl, causing the fumes to explode. But there was worse to come – when paramedics were told the cause of the accident, they laughed uncontrollably and dropped the stretcher down the stairs, breaking the man's hips and pelvis.

FILLING UP
270 million to one

Between 1993 and 2004, there were 243 explosions at Australian petrol stations sparked by static electricity discharged from the human body. One study of 150 reported 'static' fires at American gas pumps revealed that in almost all of the cases those filling up at the time were women.

There have also been several incidents where mobile phones were believed to have triggered explosions at petrol stations, including one in which an Indonesian man was severely burned and his car wrecked as he refueled while talking on his mobile.

VOLCANO
6 million to one

There are more than 1500 active volcanoes in the world and every year around 60 erupt, killing around 1000 people.

The largest active volcano in the world covers 2.2 million acres under Yellowstone National Park, in the United States. An eruption, which is already 40 000 years overdue, would destroy everything within a 900 km (600 mi) radius and kill over 25 million people.

SAUNA

40 million to one

As many as 25 people die in saunas every year. In 1997, a 61-year-old woman was found dead in the sauna of her apartment in New York. She did not have a timer to warn her that the temperature had reached 32.2°C (90°F).

And in 1999, an 88-year-old Buddhist monk and three of his followers died of heat exhaustion after spending two hours in a home-made herbal sauna in the basement of the Bungrasi temple in Bangkok.

AEROPLANE LOO WASTE

815 million to one

Passenger planes often get rid of their toilet waste by dumping it in frozen blocks. In 2005, mourners at a funeral in Motherwell, Scotland, had a lucky escape when iced toilet waste the size of a portable television hurtled to the ground as they were leaving the church, narrowly missing them.

A year earlier, a family picnic in Austria was ruined when a lump of frozen excrement fell down from the sky and landed on their barbecue, causing the grill to explode and only missing them by a few metres.

NOT GOING TO THE TOILET

550 million to one

A Californian mum died in January 2007 while trying to win the 'Hold Your Wee for a Wii' contest for a local radio competition, in which the person who drank the most water without going to the loo won a Nintendo Wii video game.

She shared the same fate as Tycho Brache, a famous Danish astronomer, whose bladder burst during a dinner party in 1601 because it would have been the height of bad manners to ask to be excused.

FACT

In March 1989, in South Carolina, prisoner Michael Anderson Godwin, who had recently had his sentence of execution by electric chair reduced to life imprisonment, died while he was sitting on the metal toilet in his cell. He had tried to fix his TV set, bit into the wire and electrocuted himself.

SCALDED BY HOT WATER

3 million to one

In the United Kingdom, around 20 people are scalded to death by hot bath water every year, and another 570 suffer serious injuries or disfigurement. In 2001, 57 Americans died from hot water accidents – more than the number of people killed by sharks in United States history.

The country with the highest rate of hot water scalding is Japan where around 150 die every year.

COW DUNG

30 million to one

In the United States, an average of 10 people a year meet a stinky end after breathing in gas from manure pits. In 1989, five dairy farm workers from Michigan died after becoming overcome by methane fumes when one of them slipped into a manure pit, and the others went in to try to rescue him.

DROWNING IN THE BATH

684 000 to one

More people drown in their own bath water than in a swimming pool, and as many children die in the bath as in the sea. In Britain, around 40 adults die in their bathtubs every year.

FACT

In 1996, a peasant woman who was boiling plums to make brandy in the Romanian village of Ruginoasa, died when the flames under her still set off a buried World War Two shell. The woman's daughter was badly injured in the explosion.

BALLPOINT PEN

40 million to one

On average, a hundred people choke to death on ballpoint pens every year – that's higher than the number of people who receive a heart-lung transplant.

In January 2007, a schoolboy from County Durham, died after a plastic pen lid got lodged in his throat while he was doing his homework.

TOOTHPICK

15 million to one

In the United States, more people choke to death on toothpicks than any other item. Most of the more than 8000 incidents and 20 fatalities happen while people are picking meat out of their teeth, or knocking back Martinis without removing the olive.

BLOWING UP A BALLOON

143 million to one

When helping with the decorations, don't blow too hard – your life could go pop before the balloon does.

In Liverpool, England, a 19-year-old-girl was blowing up balloons for a Christmas party when she suddenly suffered a brain haemorrhage by straining too hard. She died a few days later.

PLASTIC SURGERY
500 000 to one

Around 20 of every 100 000 liposuction procedures in the United States end in death – higher than the 16.4 per 100 000 mortality rate of car accidents. In 2006, budding actress Alexandra Mills, 20, died while having cosmetic surgery to correct her protruding chin, to help fulfill her dream of being on stage.

PERFUME
330 million to one

Most fragrances contain as many as 4000 different chemicals, most of which are derived from petroleum. One of the most common is toluene, which has been proven to cause cancer and nervous system damage and is designated as hazardous waste.

A teenager from Manchester, England, died in July 1998 from 'excessive deodorant use'. The 16-year-old was so obsessed with smelling good that he would spray deodorant over his entire body at least twice a day, and ended up with 10 times the lethal dosage of propane and butane in his blood. 'What a price to pay for smelling nice,' said his grieving father.

FAKE MEDICINES
4 million to one

Almost half of the medicines in developing countries are counterfeit and often either don't work or contain dangerous chemicals. According to government figures, fake medicine kills around 100 000 people in China every year.

FACT

An Australian widow chose a special way of storing her husband's ashes. After her husband was killed in a car accident in 2001, the 26-year-old had his ashes sewn into her breast implants. She said she did it so 'I'd never really have to part with him at all'.

ESCALATOR

63 million to one

In the United States, there are around 7000 escalator accidents every year. Between 1997 and 2003, there were 20 deaths on American escalators – 12 from falling and eight from getting caught in the machinery.

MANHOLE

1.5 million to one

Thousands of people fall to their deaths down open manholes in the street. In Nicaragua, where people have taken to stealing manhole covers to sell for scrap metal, over 200 die every year.

In 2005, a 56-year-old man was swept through the sewerage system for more than a kilometre after falling down a manhole when he got off his motorbike in the centre of Cannes. He eventually emerged on the other side of town, where he was found by a council worker who was unblocking storm drains.

RUN OVER BY OWN CAR

9.6 million to one

It may seem impossible, but hundreds of unfortunate motorists are run over by their own wheels every year.

In November 2006, a man died after being dragged under the tyres of his MPV as he tried to stop it rolling down his driveway in Epsom, England.

FACT

The father of the groom was killed as he videotaped the newly married couple emerging from their wedding reception in Cheshire, England. The man walked backwards out of the restaurant, taping the couple, then stepped into the street, directly into the path of a car.

FACT

A man from Cambridgeshire, England, had a real wardrobe disaster in February 2004, when it fell to the floor and pinned the door shut while he was cleaning inside. He was found dead inside the heavy wardrobe after trying to gouge his way out for a week.

WASHING MACHINE/DRYER

900 million to one

Occasionally someone gets washed, rinsed and spun off the mortal coil after getting trapped inside a washing machine or tumble dryer.

In 1999, a 39-year-old man from Virginia, tried to stuff 23 kg (50 lb) of laundry into his washing machine by climbing on top of the washer and forcing the clothes inside. He accidentally hit the washing machine's ON button, lost his balance and smashed his head against a steel beam, killing him. The machine eventually went into its high-speed spin cycle, spinning him around at about 110 km an hour (68 mph).

And in November 1988, Rafael Benitez was found spinning around in a commercial clothes dryer in Los Angeles. It is believed the 18-year-old fell inside while trying to retrieve an item of clothing. He died later in hospital.

FURNITURE

3.5 million to one

At least a hundred people are killed in the United States by their furniture every year. In 2006, a 38-year-old woman from Florida, got wedged headfirst behind her bookcase after falling while trying to fiddle with the plug of her TV set. Her family launched a massive missing persons' search, unaware that she was at home all along. It wasn't until three weeks later that they discovered her body.

YOUR CLOTHES

4.3 million to one

Beware – your clothes can kill. In 1927, famous dancer Isadora Duncan was strangulated when her long-flowing scarf snagged on the rear wheel of the sports car she was travelling in. She was dragged along the road for several metres before her chauffeur noticed what had happened.

ROAD RAGE

4 million to one

In the United States, more than 300 people are killed and over 1200 injured by enraged motorists every year. A recent survey suggests South Africa has the worst road rage offenders in the world, with 67 per cent of motorists being victims of violence or aggressive behaviour every year. The United Kingdom came second and Greece third.

BRIDGE COLLAPSE

2.3 million to one

There are over a million bridges in China, with 10 000 new ones built every year. Around 500 collapse every year, killing as many as 1000 people. Even in the United States, 150 bridges give way every year and claim around a dozen lives.

St Petersburg in Russia has 59 bridges, more than any other city in the world, some of which have also collapsed from time to time.

EXPLODING TYRE

37 million to one

Over a hundred people die worldwide when tyres unexpectedly blow up as they're being filled with air. In February 2004, a farm labourer from Gwynedd, Wales, died when a huge tractor tyre he was inflating with a compressor exploded. The coroner described his injuries as similar to those caused by a bomb blast.

FACT

Forty-four-year-old Bridget Driscoll became the first car-accident victim on 17 August 1896, when she was knocked down at London's Crystal Palace by an automobile going just seven km an hour (4.5 mph). At her inquest coroner Percy Morrison said he hoped 'such a thing would never happen again'.

FACT

A 58-year-old man of Albany, Australia, was blowing a chewing gum bubble while driving when it burst and stuck to his glasses. Blinded, he drove off the road and plunged down a hill to his death.

ROLLERCOASTER

416 million to one

They are supposed to scare you to death, but in fact fairground rides only kill around eight people every year. However, in 1998, 48 people lost their lives on rollercoasters in the United States.

The worst rollercoaster accident in Britain was in 1972 when five children were killed on the Big Dipper in Battersea, London, when one of the cars broke loose and collided with another.

SKI LIFT

800 000 to one

While half of all ski lift injuries occur at the point of getting off, half of all deaths involve mechanical failure. In 1995, two skiers were killed and eight injured on Whistler Mountain, Canada, when an emergency break activated, causing chairs to slide down the cable and slam into each other.

ELEVATOR

13 million to one

Of the 202 people who died in elevators in the United States between 1992 and 2001, 105 fell to their deaths and 44 were caught in moving parts.

In February 2005, a Greek woman got her scarf caught in the lift doors at her Athens apartment block, choking to death as the lift started going down. When a woman in the lift saw what had happened she had a heart attack and died herself.

FACT

In 1986, an American security guard was killed when, while travelling in an armoured security van, $50 000 worth of quarters fell on top of him.

FACT

In 2005, children's entertainer Marlon Pistol, known for his giant blow-up elephant Colonel Jumbo, was killed when driving along a Californian highway on his way to a party. As he sped down the freeway the six metre (20 foot) balloon elephant began to inflate, filling the cab almost instantly and causing him to crash.

PLAYING FOOTBALL

7 million to one

In 2003, Cameroon midfielder Mark-Vivien Foe died on the pitch after collapsing during the Confederations Cup semi-final against Colombia. But most of the hundreds of people who die from heart attacks while playing football every year are in non-pro games and kickarounds.

WATCHING FOOTBALL

4 million to one

On the day Holland lost to France on penalties in the 1996 European cup quarter-finals, there was a 50 per cent increase in fatal heart attacks among Dutch men. Not surprisingly, the mortality rate for women stayed the same.

SCUBA DIVING

800 000 to one

In the 10 years since January 1996, 47 people have died in scuba diving accidents and 20 in snorkelling accidents in New Zealand waters – an average of six per year. Numbers are going up as more tourists take part without proper training.

A Christchurch man brought 2005's total to five when he went diving for scallops in the Marlborough Sounds and never resurfaced.

And in 1998, Tom and Eileen Lonergan were scuba diving off Australia's Great Barrier Reef when, due to an incorrect head count, the group's boat accidentally abandoned them. Left to fend for themselves in shark-infested waters, their bodies were never recovered.

FACT

Jockey Frank Hayes had a heart attack and died during a race in 1923. His horse, Sweet Kiss, went on to win, making Hayes the only deceased jockey ever to win a race.

FACT

A Golfer from Kentucky died in July 2006 after taking a swing at a golf ball – the club broke, went through the base of his neck and pierced his aorta.

TRAMPOLINE

21 million to one

Between 1990 and 2000, trampolines bounced 11 people into the afterlife in the United States alone. In New Zealand, around 2800 people are rushed to hospital every year with trampoline injuries.

In 1994, Austrian circus dwarf Franz Dasch met his death when he bounced sideways off his trampoline straight into the mouth of Hilda the Hippo, who just happened to be yawning at the time. The crowd applauded wildly for several seconds before they realised what had happened.

SPEED BUMP

750 million to one

Road humps don't only kill your speed – they might kill you too. Eighteen-year-old Californian student Amy White was thrown from her seat and hit her head when her friend's car hit a speed bump in June 1994 – she never recovered and died three years later.

BUNGEE JUMPING

1.5 million to one

In 1991, Hal Mark Irish became the first person to die from the thrill sport bungee jumping when his cord snapped while jumping from a hot air balloon. At least five people have been killed in bungee jumping accidents every year since.

In 2000, a 22-year-old male bungee jumper met a very messy end after hurling himself off a 21 metre (70 foot) railroad trestle at Lake Accotink Park, Virginia – the rope was longer than the drop.

ELEPHANT

12 million to one

Every year, over 500 people are trampled to death by elephants, which can weigh as much as six tonnes and can run at speeds of up to 48 km an hour (29 mph).

In December 2006, a killer elephant called Osama bin Laden was shot dead by hunters in India's Assam state after killing 27 people in two years. Up to 14 people were crushed by the tuskless animal in just one month.

BULL

34 million to one

The most dangerous month to be in a field with a bull is August, when the breeding season starts. Apparently nobody told a New Zealand stock agent who was flung into the air then gored by a randy, rampaging Friesian bull in August 2006.

HIPPO

6 million to one

They may be herbivores, but hippos kill more people in Africa than any other mammal. In fact, the only animal that kills more Africans is the mosquito. The third largest land animal, the hippopotamus can weigh as much as 3175 kg (7000 lb) and, when scared, charges at 32 km an hour (20 mph).

FACT

In 2002, a pensioner died after being attacked by a flock of angry seagulls. The gulls swooped on the 80-year-old after he disturbed a nest of chicks as he cleaned the roof of his home in Anglesey, north Wales. They knocked him to the ground and continued to peck him as he lay unconscious.

FACT

The flea is the biggest human killer of all time. Though tiny and wingless, it is an external parasite responsible for plagues that have killed 75 million people worldwide. A female flea can consume up to 15 times her own body weight in blood each day.

CROCODILE

3 million to one

Crocodiles kill over 2000 people every year. A croc's closing jaw exerts about 700 kg (1540 lb) of pressure – 40 times more than a human jaw.

The most deaths in a single attack was in 1945, when 900 Japanese soldiers crossed through 16 km (10 mi) of croc-infested mangrove swamps to escape the Royal Navy. Only 500 managed to make it to the other side.

FROG

570 million to one

Some of the Poison Arrow frogs of South America have enough toxins in them to kill 2200 people instantly. Members of the jungle tribes, who collect the poison to tip their arrows, make up most of their human victims.

SNAKE BITE

500 000 to one

Snakes kill an estimated 125 000 people a year. The African Black Mamba, with a coffin-shaped head, is the deadliest snake in the world – one bite can carry enough venom to kill 40 humans.

More people die from snake bites in India than in any other country in the world, more than 20 000 fatalities every year.

PUFFER FISH

92 Million to one

Here's a dish that really puts the 'die' into dining. As well as being a Japanese delicacy, the puffer fish is also one of the world's most poisonous fish and kills around 100 restaurant-goers every year. The skin, ovaries, intestines and liver of the fish contain tetrodotoxin, which is more toxic than cyanide and for which there is no known antidote. Only specially trained and licensed chefs can prepare it, as a slip of the knife that accidently releases the minutest amount of the poison into the food, means almost certain death.

FACT

A 40-year-old golfer of Clondalkin, Ireland, was killed by a rat
which ran up his trouser leg and urinated on him while he hunted
for a lost ball at Caddockstown golf course in County Kildare.
Doctors believe that the deadly Weil's Disease carried by the
rat was passed from the victim's fingers to his mouth, when he
touched his leg then smoked a cigar.

53

SPIDER

22 million to one

Despite their fearsome reputation, less than a hundred people die from spider bites every year. Most are from the Black Widow, whose venom is more powerful than the rattlesnake's.

In 2004, three women died after visiting the same bathroom of a Florida restaurant, where a two-striped Telamonia spider lurking under the toilet seat had bitten them on the backside.

KILLER BEES

32 million to one

Once Africanized bees get angry they stay mad for a whole day, attacking people and animals for up to 400 m (0.25 mi) from the nest inflicting over 1000 stings in a single attack. These bees kill around a hundred people every year.

In August 2006, a 39-year-old man from Arizona died after being stung over 300 times when he disturbed a hive on his roof. The average human can tolerate a hundred strings.

ANTS

890 million to one

African driver ants attack in their millions and can devour a tethered horse in a matter of hours. Only a few – mostly drunk – humans have been known to have died in this way, while swarms of the hungry insects have even been used to execute criminals.

55

PIRANHA
33 million to one

The piranha is the world's most ferocious freshwater fish. With razor-sharp teeth capable of devouring 16 cm (6 in) of flesh with each bite, a shoal is capable of stripping and eating even large prey in a matter of seconds.

In September 1981, a shoal of piranhas is believed to have devoured up to 300 people when a boat capsized and sank near Obidos, Brazil.

JELLYFISH
80 million to one

Jellyfish kill more people than sharks every year. The most deadly is the Box Jellyfish whose sting can kill a human in just three minutes. It has caused at least 63 recorded deaths since 1884.

In 2002, a 58-year-old wealthy British tycoon became the first person to be killed by the thumbnail-sized Irukandji Jellyfish. It stung him as he swam in waters off the Queensland coast, Australia.

SHARK
256 million to one

Since 1530, there have only been around 2000 confirmed shark attacks around the world, with less than a hundred deaths. But the numbers are rising as more people take holidays on coasts where sharks live and now sharks kill around 10 people a year.

The most vicious shark is the bull shark, which has the highest level of testosterone of any animal on the planet, even more than a stampeding elephant.

FACT

In 1994, Belgian farmer Frans Jaumotte was found dead and mutilated in his henhouse – he had run out of chicken feed and the hungry chickens had attacked him, pecking out his eyes and heart.

57

FACT

In July 2001, two Papua New Guinea fishermen bled to death after their penises were bitten off by Pacu fish while standing waist deep in a river. The killer fish, a relative of the piranha, follow a trail of urine in the water, swim to its source and then bite it off with razor-sharp teeth.

FISH

690 million to one

Cases of fish exacting revenge on anglers by jumping into their throats and choking them to death are strangely common.

In 2003, Cambodian student Lim Vanthan was proudly showing his parents the prized 20 cm-long (8 in) fish he had when it suddenly jumped from his basket and lodged in his throat.

And in 2005, eight-year-old Samiun Ahmad from Malaysia was holding a 7 cm-long (3 in) perch he'd caught in a neighbour's pond when it jumped out of his hands and into his mouth, choking him to death. Friends tried to pull the fish out of his mouth but it had lodged itself firmly.

DOG

3.5 million to one

A bite from a vicious dog sends a person to the hospital every 40 seconds. In the United States there are 17 fatal dog attacks every year, while worldwide more than 55 000 people die from rabies, mostly caused by dog bites.

And if your dog's the softest, friendliest mutt in the world, don't assume you're safe. In 1999, an American man was giving his mother a gun safety lesson when his white French Poodle Benji jumped on his lap, pulled the trigger on his .45 pistol and shot him through the heart – then affectionately licked his face as he bled to death.

ZOO ANIMALS

33 million to one

You're more likely to be trampled by an elephant at the zoo than ripped apart in the lion enclosure. In October 2001, horrified visitors to London Zoo saw an elephant crush a senior elephant keeper by stepping on him after he had tripped and fallen.

In 2005, a Polish woman was mauled to death by bears after she fell into their zoo enclosure in the city of Chorzow.

FREAK WAVE

21 million to one

Massive waves up to 30 m (98 ft) high have been know to rise from apparently calm seas, sinking dozens of ships every year. In 1978, the 43 000-tonne cargo ship *Munchen* sank along with all hands after being struck by a huge force, thought to be a rogue wave.

Even people on land can be suddenly dragged into the sea by a freak wave. In March 2005, a 6 m (20 ft) wave washed over a funeral party on Gran Canaria, in the Canary Islands, that had gathered on a cliff to spread the ashes of a 16-year-old boy. The boy's dad and uncle were swept away and drowned.

CRAMP

6.7 million to one

It is excruciating at the best of times, but getting a bout of cramp while swimming can be fatal. In 2002, a 25-year-old Scottish backpacker plucked up the courage to swim across a crocodile-infested river in Australia. The crocs didn't get him, but he drowned after getting cramp halfway.

STINGRAY

3.5 billion to one

Only 17 people have been killed by stingrays in the last decade. In September 2006, TV's crocodile hunter Steve Irwin died when a ray punctured his heart as he swam off Australia's coast. A month later, a pensioner in Florida was left fighting for his life after a ray leapt onto his boat, leaving a 30 cm (1 ft) toxic barb piercing his heart.

FACT

In 1985, a group of lifeguards in New Orleans decided to have a party to celebrate an entire season without any drownings. At the end of the party one of the guests was found dead at the bottom of the swimming pool.

MUD
10 million to one

When an American man was stopped by police in January 2007 for having an out-of-date car registration, he fled into a field. He then got stuck in a mud hole and died of hypothermia. Deputies searched for an hour before finding him.

Every year, mudslides kill around 25 people in the United States – mostly those rich enough to live on the Los Angeles hillsides – as well as thousands of people in developing countries.

BURIED ALIVE
48 million to one

At least 1000 people die every year after holes they are digging cave in on them. Beachgoers make up many of the victims, like teenager Layton Shepley, who was buried under a tonne of sand in January 2004, while digging a tunnel between two metre-deep holes on a beach near Ocean Grove, Australia.

In January 2006, a 46-year-old dad-of-two, died under a huge mound of earth while digging for Victorian bottles in County Durham, England.

AVALANCHE
10 000 to one (for skiers)

Over a million snow avalanches tumble down mountainsides every year. Reaching speeds of up to 394 km an hour (245 mph), they kill more than 200 people a year, with most fatalities in the European Alps.

Most victims suffocate within minutes, but a quarter die from hitting trees and rocks on the way down. Only two per cent live long enough to die from hypothermia.

FACT

In 1919, a huge tank at a Boston confectionery factory burst, sending a wave of molasses treacle flowing down the streets at an estimated 56 km an hour (35 mph), killing 21 people and injuring 150. It took five years to remove the treacle from the cobbled streets, and residents claim they can still smell it on hot summer days.

FALLING COCONUT

250 million to one

Coconuts kill around 150 people every year, 15 times more than sharks. Falling from a height of 24 m (80 feet), they can build up an impact speed of 80 km an hour (50 mph) and a force of as much as 1000 kg (2205 lbs).

GOLF BALL

83 million to one

Stray golf balls injure and kill hundreds every year. In February 2005, a 67-year-old man from Texas died when his son hit a golf ball which bounced off a tree and struck him on the head. 'It was just the way God wanted him to go to heaven,' his son later said.

ICICLE

366 million to one

Icicles falling from tall buildings kill several people every year. In 1998, Moscow student Elizaveta Rolshchikova won NZD$7300 (USD$5000) damages for the wrongful death of his mother, who was impaled by a large icicle as she walked along a city street. Two years later, the family of a Chicago man, killed by a human torso-sized icicle that fell from a rooftop, won a suit for NZD$6.6 million (USD$4.5 million).

HURRICANE
6 million to one

A hurricane releases more energy in 10 minutes than all the world's nuclear weapons combined. Thanks to global warming there is an average of 18 severe hurricanes a year, compared with just 10 in the 1970s. The strongest hurricane ever recorded was Hurricane Wilma in October 2005, which devastated parts of the Florida coast with 266 km an hour (165 mph) winds.

GIANT HAILSTONES
200 million to one

In 2002, hailstones the size of eggs killed 25 people and injured more than 200 in the Henan province of China.

The heaviest hailstones on record weighed up to a kilo (2.2 lb) and fell at a rate of more than 160 km an hour (100 mph) in Bangladesh in 1986, killing 92 people.

In 2004, it was discovered that a group of 200 nomads dating back from the ninth century, whose frozen corpses were discovered beside a lake in the Himalayas, were actually killed by one of the most lethal hailstorms in history.

EARTHQUAKE
600 000 to one

Each year, several million earthquakes occur around the world, of which about 60 are classified as significant and 19 as major (of magnitude 7.0 or higher).

The most catastrophic earthquake in 400 years happened on 27 July 1976 in Tangshan, China, leaving 255 000 dead and 800 000 injured. In recorded history it is estimated that earthquakes have killed around 75 million people.

FACT

In 1902, the catastrophic eruption of Mt Pelee in the Caribbean island of Martinique completely wiped out the town of St Pierre, around six km (four mi) away, and killed around 40 000 people. The only survivor was Ludger Sylbaris, a prisoner in the town's underground dungeon, who was later pardoned.

RADIATION

19 million to one

An accident at your local nuclear power plant is the least likely way you might end up exposed to deadly levels of radiation.

In December 2006, over 120 people in London were exposed to the radioactive poison polonium-210 which killed ex-Russian spy Alexander Litvinenko. Of those, 12 people were at levels that could pose health risks.

And in 1989, a small capsule containing highly radioactive isotope Cesium-137 was found inside the concrete wall of an apartment building in Kramatorsk, Ukraine. The capsule had been lost in the 1970s and ended up mixed with gravel used to construct that building in 1980. By the time the capsule was discovered, six residents of the building had died from leukaemia.

TSUNAMI

1.6 million to one

Around 1000 tsunamis are recorded around the world every year. The waves can reach as high as 30 m (98 ft) and can travel at 950 km an hour (590 mph) – as fast as a passenger jet.

In Japan, there have been 195 tsunamis over a 1313 year period, averaging one event every 6.7 years, the highest rate of occurrence in the world.

SNEEZING

770 million to one

At around 160 km an hour (100 mph), the force of a typical sneeze can cause serious injury or even death. In July 2006, a Welsh teenager collapsed and died of a brain haemorrhage after a sneezing fit, while on a camping holiday with his family.

EATEN BY CANNIBALS

25 billion to one

You're pretty unlikely to get ritually consumed these days. The Korowai tribe of Papua New Guinea is believed to be the last cannibal tribe left on earth.

But you might still end up filling someone's stomach – when Flight 571 crashed into the Andes in October 1972, survivors resorted to eating the deceased to stay alive. Scientists have found that a man weighing 68 kg (150 lb) would make a meal for about 75 people.

SPONTANEOUS COMBUSTION

8 billion to one

In the last 300 years more than 200 people have reportedly burnt to a crisp for no apparent reason.

In 1951, Mary Hardy Reeser was reduced to nothing more than a smouldering pile of ash in her living room. All that remained of the pensioner was her left foot and her skull.

PREMATURE BURIAL

510 million to one

Throughout history people have been accidentally pronounced dead, buried then woken up six feet under, only to die for real from lack of oxygen. It happens occasionally even today, prompting one Italian coffin manufacturer to introduce a model with an intercom and beeper system.

In 1993, Sipho Mdletshe was declared dead after a traffic accident in Johannesburg, South Africa, and then spent two days in a metal box in a mortuary before his cries alerted staff. Afterwards his fiancée refused to see him, thinking he was a zombie who had returned from the dead to haunt her.

FACT

In the early 17th century, Marjorie Elphinsone died and was buried in Ardtannies, Scotland. When grave robbers attempted to steal the jewellery interred with her, she started groaning and they fled for their lives. Marjorie then walked home and outlived her husband by six years.

SUICIDE BOMBER

5.3 million to one

In 2005, there were 11 000 terrorist attacks killing more than 14 000 civilians, including 360 suicide bombings which claimed 3000 lives. But while terrorism tops the list of things Americans are most afraid of, during that year only 56 of the victims were US citizens.

EXECUTED BY THE STATE

400 million to one

Around 13 000 people have been legally executed in the United States, and DNA testing now proves that at least a hundred were innocent of any crime. In countries like Saudi Arabia you can still get the death penalty for crimes such as adultery, homosexuality and converting to Christianity.

CULT SUICIDE

30 million to one

Over 200 000 people are lured into doomsday cults every year. Perhaps the strangest was in March 1997, when 39 members of the crazy Heaven's Gate cult committed suicide in a San Diego mansion in a bizarre attempt to board an alien spaceship they believed was trailing the Hale Bop comet. They'd even each packed a suitcase and had five dollars worth of quarters in their pockets to use on the UFO's slot machines.

The largest cult suicide happened on 17 March 2000 when as many as 1000 members of a Ugandan doomsday cult killed themselves in a fire. The group believed the world was corrupt, but curiously had a feast that involved largest quantities of Coca-Cola and beef before dying.

FACT

In September 1985, two brothers-in-law in Vallefiorita, Italy, began to fight about who would get the last free space in the family tomb. The dispute reached a head when one of the men stabbed the other to death, and subsequently lost the vacancy to his victim.

FACT

John Sedgwick, a famous Union General in the US civil war, was killed by a Confederate sharpshooter as he stood on a hilltop in May 1864, immediately prior to the battle of Spotsylvania Court House. His last words were: 'They couldn't hit an elephant from this dis . . .'

PENGUIN BOOKS

Published by the Penguin Group

Penguin Group (NZ), 67 Apollo Drive, Rosedale,
North Shore 0632, New Zealand (a division of Pearson New Zealand Ltd)
Penguin Group (USA) Inc., 375 Hudson Street,
New York, New York 10014, USA
Penguin Group (Canada), 90 Eglinton Avenue East, Suite 700, Toronto,
Ontario, M4P 2Y3, Canada (a division of Pearson Penguin Canada Inc.)
Penguin Books Ltd, 80 Strand, London, WC2R 0RL, England
Penguin Ireland, 25 St Stephen's Green,
Dublin 2, Ireland (a division of Penguin Books Ltd)
Penguin Group (Australia), 250 Camberwell Road, Camberwell,
Victoria 3124, Australia (a division of Pearson Australia Group Pty Ltd)
Penguin Books India Pvt Ltd, 11, Community Centre,
Panchsheel Park, New Delhi – 110 017, India
Penguin Books (South Africa) (Pty) Ltd, 24 Sturdee Avenue,
Rosebank, Johannesburg 2196, South Africa

Penguin Books Ltd, Registered Offices: 80 Strand, London, WC2R 0RL, England

First published by Penguin Group (NZ), 2007
3 5 7 9 10 8 6 4 2

Designed and typeset by Keely O'Shannessy
Illustrations by Elliot Stewart
Printed by Everbest Printing Co. Ltd, China

ISBN: 978 0 14 30070 6 7
A catalogue record for this book is available
from the National Library of New Zealand.

www.penguin.co.nz

FACT

In 2001, Michael Franklin was killed by his own body gasses. An autopsy showed he had died in his sleep from breathing in the poisonous cloud that was hanging over his bed, produced by his diet of beans and cabbage. Even three of the men who went in to rescue him had to be treated.

FRIGHT

50 million to one

Being scared causes the heart to speed up, which for some people can lead to fibrillation, a non-rhythmic quivering of the heart, which may result in death.

In December 2006, a British teenager was literally scared to death when her mobile phone alarm went off unexpectedly. And in 1983, the daughter of New Yorker Mrs Corson, presumed dead due to heart disease, died of fright when her mother suddenly sat up in her coffin.

HICCUPS

9.5 billion to one

The world record for hiccupping is held by a farmer from Iowa, who apparently hiccupped for more than 60 years for no known reason. But in rare cases, hiccups can be fatal, like Pope Pius XII, who died after a bout of uncontrollable hiccups in 1958.

LAUGHTER

15 billion to one

There have been at least two documented instances of people laughing themselves to death. In 1975, bricklayer Alex Mitchell from King's Lynn, England, found an episode of the TV comedy show *The Goodies* so hilarious he laughed continuously for 25 minutes before slumping dead on his sofa. His widow later sent *The Goodies* a letter thanking them for making Alex's final moments so pleasant.

FACT

An 80-year-old New Jersey pharmacist had often said that when his time came he would take himself to the funeral home, where he had a pre-arranged burial contract. In 2001, he did just that, waiting behind the wheel of his car until he died of natural causes.

FACT

At a funeral in Lyon, France, 57-year-old Claudia Sassi died of shock at her husband's funeral after she heard her husband's voice coming from the coffin shouting, 'Let me out!'

What she didn't know was that the voice belonged to a fellow mourner, Jacques de Putron, who was a ventriloquist. A distraught de Putron later stated, 'I thought that it would cheer everyone up and make them feel better!'